Cartoons to cheer up a
STROPPY
MARE

by The Odd Squad

CARTOONS TO CHEER UP A STROPPY MARE

© 2011 by Allan Penderleith

All rights reserved

First published in 2011 by

Ravette Publishing Limited

PO Box 876, Horsham, West Sussex RH12 9GH

ISBN: 978-1-84161-361-1

Patsy's mate was always on Twitter.

Maude loves a guy with tight buns.

Maude was a real back seat driver.

Lily makes an apple puff.

Suddenly Maude regretted getting botox.

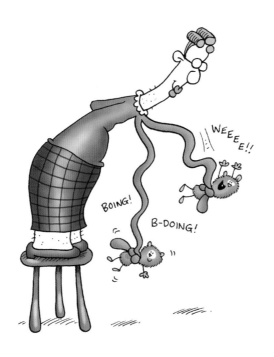

Saggy boobs make great bungee ropes
for bored hamsters.

Maude got a belly button stud.

Maude took the kids to the farm to
see an egg getting laid.

Suddenly Maude realised she had
ordered the wrong birthday cake.

For lunch, Maude bought the duck wrap.

It was time to clear out her handbag.

Jeff didn't approve of Maude's GI diet.

Jeff has asked Maude to
fill the car up.

No-one had the heart to tell Lily
it was just a mushroom.

Maude loved doggy fashion.

The strawberries Maude picked
were completely tasteless.

Brenda always had safe sex.

Theresa's roots were showing again.

Once again, a night out with Jean
ends in disappointment.

As a louder and more satisfying
alternative to clapping, Lily uses her
bingo wings.

Maude goes out dressed on
a shoestring.

Maude had warned the cat not
to lick itself so much.

Suddenly Maude realised she
was wearing the wrong panty liner.

Maude sent her salad back for
being too herby.

Never apply lipstick when you have hiccups.

At the weekend, Maude's hubbie
becomes Iron Man!

Barbara started having hot flushes.

As a treat for Jeff, Maude tries on
something see-through.

Dug had asked Patsy to see her chuff.

Maude had asked Jeff for an iTouch.

Maude's new bra came with added lift.

When they arrived at the restaurant
their table wasn't ready.

Debbie loves a good hard banging.

As it was a cold evening,
Lily chucks on some more coal.

Maude finds an embarrassing ladder
in her tights.

Patsy arrived in casualty with something stuck in her throat.

Other ODD SQUAD gift books available ...

	ISBN	PRICE
Cartoons to Cheer up a Grumpy Old Git	978-1-84161-360-4	£4.99
I Love Beer	978-1-84161-238-6	£5.99
I Love Dad	978-1-84161-252-2	£5.99
I Love Mum	978-1-84161-249-2	£5.99
I Love Poo	978-1-84161-240-9	£5.99
I Love Sex	978-1-84161-241-6	£4.99
I Love Wine	978-1-84161-239-3	£4.99
I Love Xmas	978-1-84161-262-1	£4.99
Little Book of Booze	978-1-84161-138-9	£2.99
Little Book of Men	978-1-84161-093-1	£2.99
Little Book of Pumping	978-1-84161-140-2	£2.50
Little Book of Sex	978-1-84161-095-5	£2.99
Little Book of X-rated Cartoons	978-1-84161-141-9	£2.99

HOW TO ORDER:

Please send a cheque/postal order in £ sterling, made payable to 'Ravette Publishing' for the cover price of the book/s and allow the following for post & packing ...

UK & BFPO	70p for the first book & 40p per book thereafter
Europe & Eire	£1.30 for the first book & 70p per book thereafter
Rest of the world	£2.20 for the first book & £1.10 per book thereafter

RAVETTE PUBLISHING LTD
PO Box 876, Horsham, West Sussex RH12 9GH
Tel: 01403 711443   Fax: 01403 711554   Email: ingrid@ravettepub.co.uk

Prices and availability are subject to change without prior notice